This book belongs to

_____

About the Author

Christina Trevino is a Leadership trainer, speaker and personal development coach who has worked with clients of all ages, from disadvantaged youth to corporate professionals. She holds a Bachelor Degree in Social Sciences as well as certifications in Communication, Team Building and Critical Preventative Intervention.

Christina recognizes that many emotional and behavioral frustrations stem from a lack of information and a process for healthy expression.

She knows how important it is to establish a nurturing environment for emotional development as early as possible.

The Zoo In YOU is a program that builds greater awareness about emotions and how they constructively or destructively impact our relationships.

The Zoo In You Copyright © 2024
All rights reserved. This book may not be reproduced or transmitted in whole or in part, in any form or by any means without written permission of the author and publisher.

Published by: Zoo In You LLC
Austin, TX 78703
http://www.thezooinyou.com

Author: Christina Trevino
Illustrated by: Sara Lee Cely & Sourav Majumder

ISBN: 978-0-9837658-6-8 (hardcover, revised)
ISBN: 978-0-9837658-7-5 (paperback, revised)
ISBN: 978-0-9837658-8-2 (e-book, revised)

For Katie and Amanda,
who inspire my zoo keeper to find the calm inside my zoo.

An emotion is not who you are.
An emotion is just where you are.

The Zoo is fun! It's a learning game.
You'll meet each emotion, and know them by name.

My name is
Sami,
I've had a
rough day.

It started out fun;
**we all went
to play.**

I found a
new toy,
and I thought it looked fun.

Sara tried to **take it** but I wasn't quite **done.**

She got
mad at me,
and grabbed at
my hand.

I pulled it away
and took a
firm stand.

Then we were **rolling** and yelling out loud.

Everyone came running;
we were drawing
a crowd.

Our parents said we were **out of control,** like monkeys gone mad.

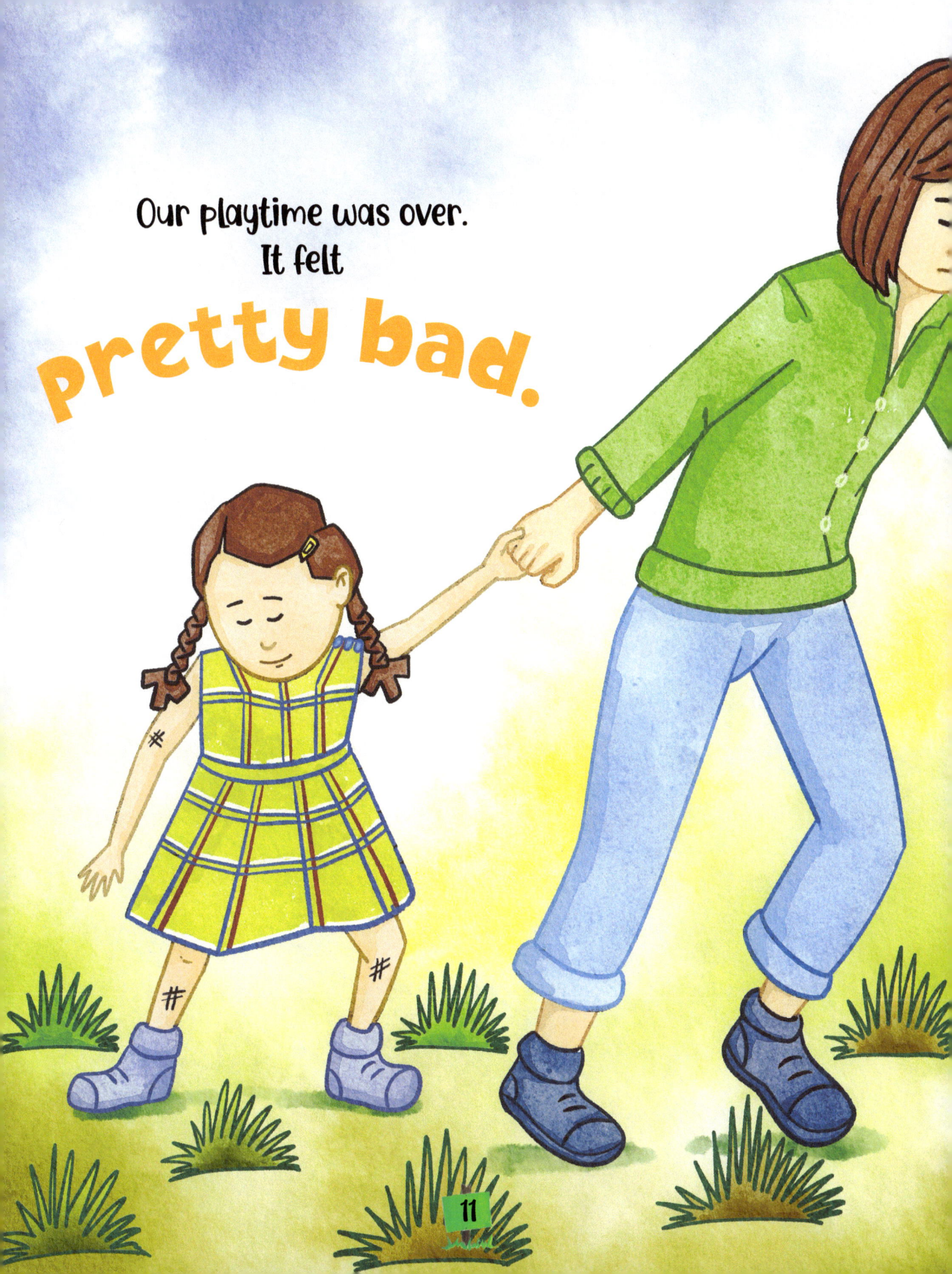

I don't know what happened;
something fills up
the space.
WHERE do you learn nice?
Is there such a place?

SCARED JOY ANGRY GRIEF HAPPY MAD CAUTION SAD

As I sit and think, something comes **into view.**

What's that ahead? It looks like a **Zoo?**

I can hear a song
coming from the zoo,
a song of emotions,
with an animal crew.

Hello! someone says.
Are you brand new?
Allow me to welcome you
to The Zoo In YOU!

Emotions

Scared

Sad

Angry

Happy

The zoo is the place **emotions** are found.

Soon you'll learn **your way** around.

Let's get going!
I'll be your trusty guide.
My name is

Hugzy;

I'm here by your side.

Emotions and animals,
that's what we're sharing.
They're teamed up
in a helpful pairing.

We'll meet all sorts of
animals in this zoo,
animals that have emotions
to share with you.

Emotions are friends,
and it's okay if
they're wild;
they're all brand new
when you're a child.

You're the Keeper of the Zoo in YOU.
You get the keys and hat.
Now you have
the power.
Be careful with that!

As you start down this path,
with animals abound,
you're the mighty
Zoo Keeper;
you're safe and you're sound.

Meet Hucky the ducky.
He has a wise point of view.
He teaches

happy;

his outlook is new.

Sometimes you're **happy** in every way.

Sometimes happy is just a small part of your day.

Meet Tabitha the tiger.

She'll teach **anger** to you.

Anger can be **useful** when you know what to do.

When you feel **angry,** you might POUND on the door.

When you feel **angry,** you might **fall** to the floor.

I'm Shay the donkey.
I'll tell you about
sad.

It comes and goes.
It's not
good or bad.

When you feel **sad,** tears may come to **your eyes.**

When you feel
sad,
you may not want
to try.

Now take
a few
breaths;

It's Marti the mouse.

He'll teach **scared** from inside his house.

There are times you'll feel
cautious
and times you'll feel
scared.
I'll teach the difference;
soon you'll be prepared.

Let's go to
Recovery Park;
you'll feel like new.
You'll find
the calm
inside your Zoo.

Now I know what happened to me.

Big emotions made it hard to see.

They came on **strong** and took over the scene.

I was feeling pulled between **nice and mean.**

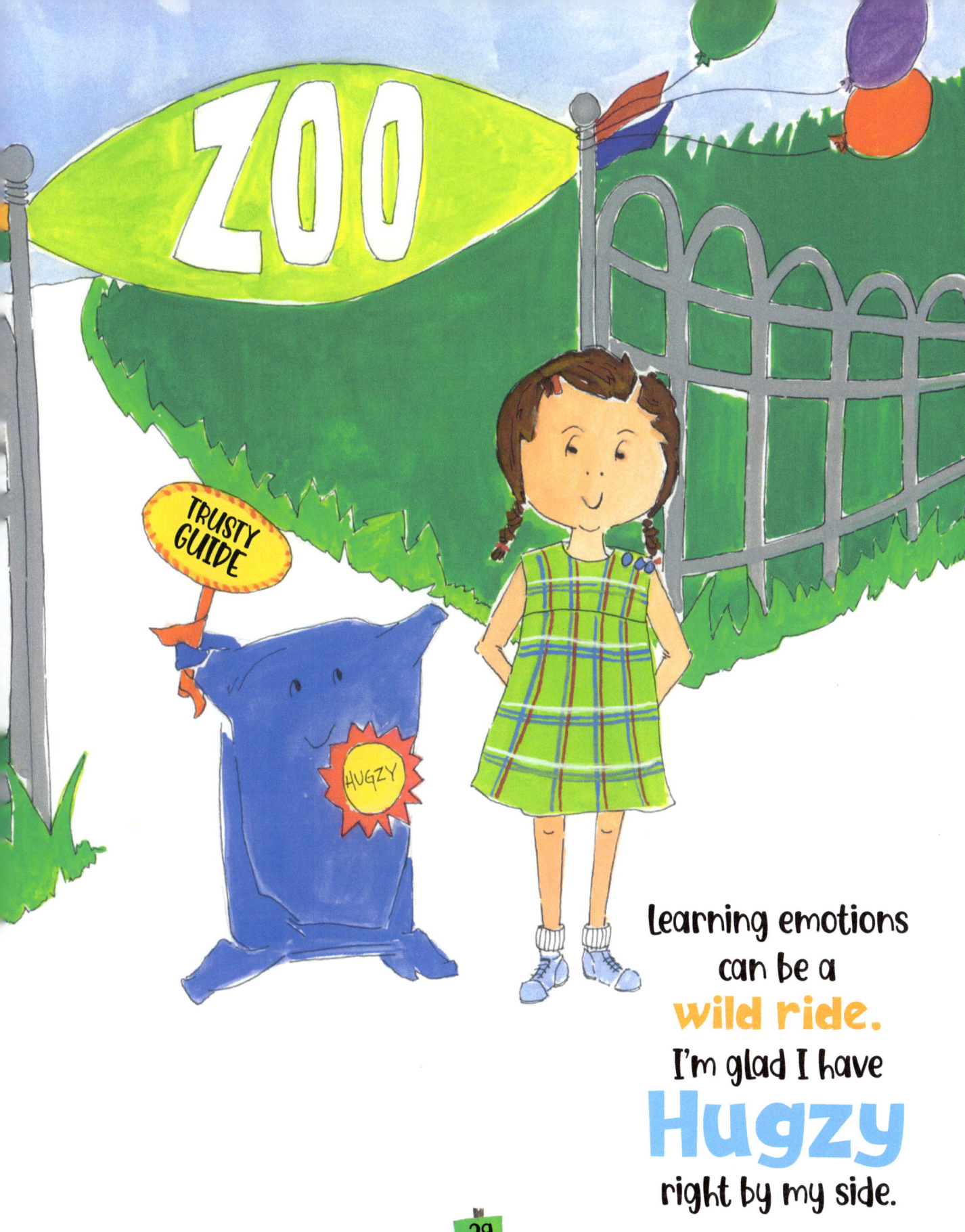

Exploring emotions is fun to do.
You're the mighty zoo keeper at the **Zoo In You.**

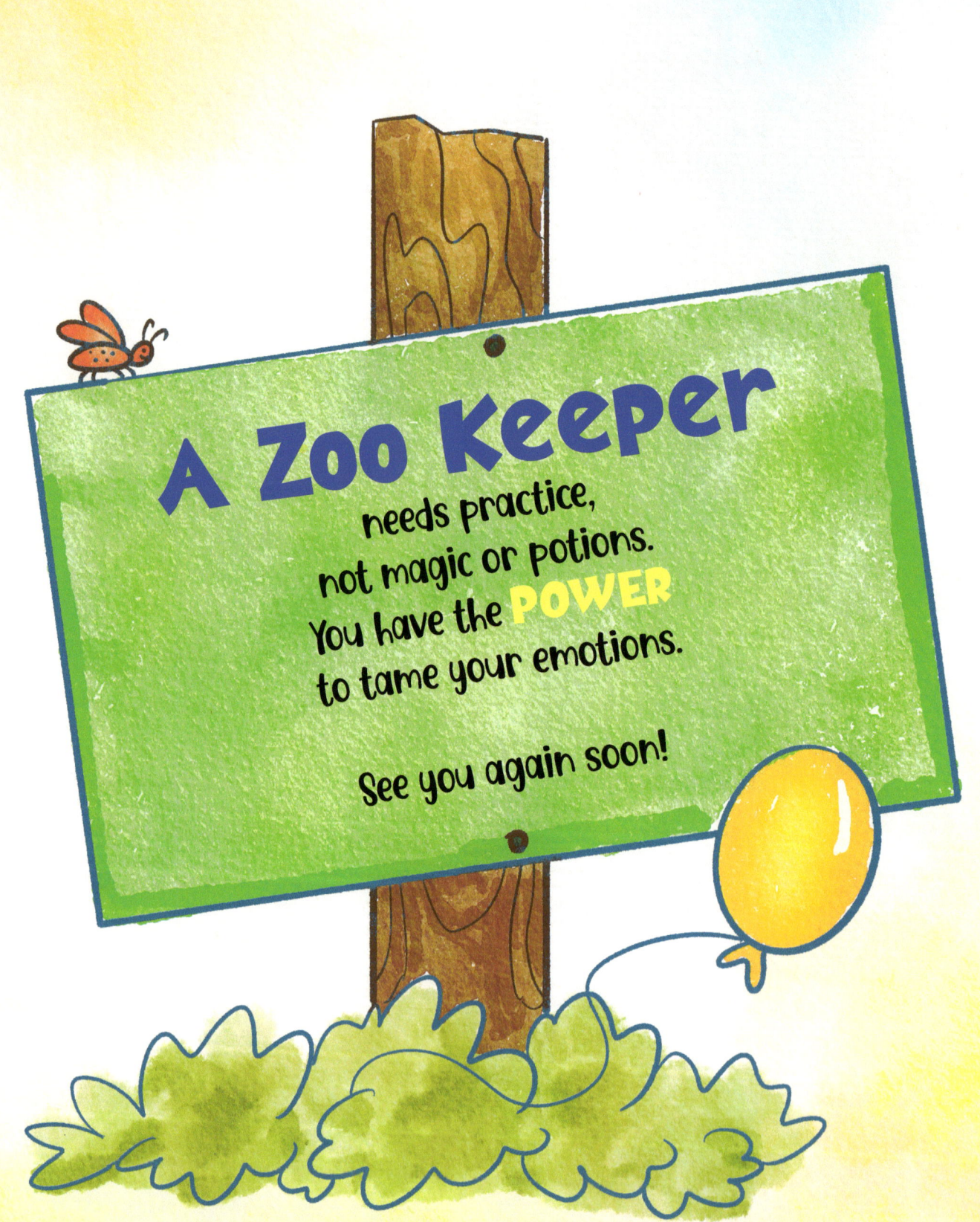

www.ingramcontent.com/pod-product-compliance
Lightning Source LLC
Chambersburg PA
CBHW042141290426
44110CB00002B/73